Motivation Quotes:

92 Affirmations For Immediate Motivational Success Using Motivational Words And Motivational Thoughts

By Gary Vurnum

www.92Tips.com and www.Vurnum.com

Motivation Quotes: 92 Affirmations For
Immediate Motivational Success Using
Motivational Words And Motivational
Thoughts
ISBN: 1450550029
EAN-13: 9781450550024

For Katie, Skye, and Connor

"The only person stopping you is you! You've only got one shot at life so you might as well just go for it and see what happens."

"Want To Achieve ANY Goal You Set? The FREE 6 Essential Steps To Achieve ANY Goal Special Report Will Show You How..."

FREE

In this Special Report you will discover...

- Exactly how many goals you should be aiming for at any one time.

- Why just visualizing your goals will have ZERO effect on whether you achieve them or not!

- Why putting your goal where you can see it all the time is a recipe for failure.

- Why the 'experts' have got it all wrong about whether you should tell people your goals or not.

- PLUS a special gift worth up to $120!

Go to www.GoalAchievementFormula.com/free

If I focus on merely meeting expectations, I will not perform at my best.

1

But when I give my mind room to run free, I excel beyond my wildest dreams.

I can slay expectations because I am daring.

2

My creativity is a force to be reckoned with and my organizational skills help me to be efficient. I truly have uncontainable talent!

I work for the passion and not for the expectations.

3

I remove mythical expectations from the forefront of my thoughts in order to work with passion. Passion gives me the drive to achieve. For me, the journey is the reward.

I remove stagnation and add motivation to tip the scale of time management in my favor.

4

My time management skills weigh in with a lot more benefits when I replace the activities that waste my time with the things that inspire me.

I recognize that stress and worry are the heaviest causes of getting stuck.

5

They waste my time, distract my focus, and turn productive energy into harmful effects. The more stress and worry I can remove, the better off I am.

I choose to replace worry with optimism and a joyful outlook on life.

6

When I know deep down that everything will turn out for the best, I have less stress. When I remember to look for the silver lining, I am choosing to appreciate the best that life has to offer.

I never get bored doing the same tasks as I use my creativity to do them differently each time.

7

This challenges my mind to come up with fun ways of doing them and keeps me energetic and excited about lackluster chores.

It is in my nature to impress and to perform above the rest.

8

If I don't feel like I have the strength to finish something I've started, a little dose of pressure clears up my view quickly.

I accept that there are times when distractions are necessary.

9

When this happens, I take care of the situation promptly and get right back to my task. As before, I tackle an easy item first to refocus and rebuild momentum.

If I am always pouring myself out, I will run dry.

10

To renew my strength and be a better worker, I need to take breaks. It is okay to stop and rest. Resting does not make me lazy or irresponsible. On the other hand, when I rest, I demonstrate maturity.

It is such a relief to be organized.

11

The systems I have in my life make my daily chores more manageable. I am able to classify projects and accomplish them in a sensible way.

It is wise and reasonable to recognize when the load is too heavy.

12

I never put work above personal health. Trying to do everything alone is a sign of selfish immaturity. I cannot possibly believe that I am the only person that can get the job done well.

Others enjoy working with me because I make them feel valued.

13

I support the people working with me and I make myself available for questions and suggestions. Ultimately, my work benefits from the creativity of others and I can get quality work done without exhaustion.

I make good use of my time.

14

By remaining in the moment and focusing on the task at hand, I optimize my productivity.

At the beginning of each day, I make a list of things I need to remember.

15

Then, because I am confident that important matters won't be forgotten, I let go of thoughts that I would otherwise need to keep juggling.

I minimize outside distractions.

16

While I have grown so accustomed to phone and email that I can hardly imagine life without them, I can turn them off from time to time for my own good! They are merely tools and should be treated as such.

Although distractions may arise every day, these petty diversions do not tempt me.

17

I dismiss distractions because they steer me off course. My direction is deliberate. Choosing to stay on track is a good decision.

I take pleasure in thinking about the future with intense anticipation.

18

I plan ahead to keep myself at an advantage over uncertainty. Planning ahead helps me cultivate great ideas that may not come to me when I am placed in the spotlight.

I fully let go of trying to remember everything.

19

It feels good to write down important items for safe keeping.

Writing down the important things in my life gives me freedom.

20

It frees my mind from unnecessary clutter and stress, and leaves room for more significant thoughts. It frees me from wasted time and allows me more time for pleasure.

I have clear boundaries for my work because I want to enjoy the other aspects of my life.

21

No matter how hard I labor, work will always be there. I keep work separate from my personal life.

In my list of priorities, relationships always come first.

22

I am not in a relationship with my job. My family always comes before my work. When I spend time with my family, all thoughts of work are squeezed out of my mind.

I need time for myself so I don't lose my identity.

23

Taking time for myself helps me recharge so I can continue to be happy, healthy and productive. During my time-off, I am creative and I pursue my other passions because it rejuvenates me.

Life is all about balance.

24

My soul needs a balanced diet just like my body. Allowing myself an occasional sweet treat helps me to stay on track.

Consistent action and good time management skills keep me focused on where I want to go.

25

Therefore, I take the time to plan my day according to my priorities and then follow my schedule to the best of my ability.

Constant activity enables me to be productive.

26

One of the laws of physics states that a body in motion tends to stay in motion, while a body at rest tends to stay at rest. It takes more energy to get a body at rest going again than it does to just keep it going.

Change is a natural part of life.

27

Those who adapt, thrive. Those who don't, become extinct! I choose to thrive, to use change to help me grow and learn, and to take advantage of new opportunities to help me succeed.

When challenges arise, I adjust my path to accommodate them.

28

I take time to seek solutions and then act decisively on my decision, adapting to the new circumstances without flinching.

I let go of the tendency to resist something just because it is a change from what I am used to.

29

Instead, I re-make my plans to take advantage of the benefits these new changes can bring.

On my daily schedule, I leave some wiggle room.

30

This gives me the time to break away from the normal daily tasks to handle distractions without putting me behind schedule. I find that I am well prepared for distractions and can easily get right back on track.

Managing my time well gives me the time to keep myself healthy, both mentally and physically.

31

It allows for variety and excitement and it keeps me alert to new possibilities.

No matter what the challenge is before me, I am ready to leap over it.

32

I welcome all forms of pressure including competition, deadlines, evaluations, and high expectations.

Being on time shows that I am mature and responsible.

33

I gain the respect of my colleagues and my family's trust when I am on time.

I live for challenges.

34

My life would be a monotonous and predictable Ferris- wheel without the gift of new experiences. I push myself by looking for opportunities to improve myself and my community.

I let go of the desire to impress others with my skills or speed.

35

I keep my eye on my goal, set a pace I am confident I can maintain, and then I begin. I know I will have the time and energy to accomplish what I set out to do by consistently moving forward.

Feeling productive boosts my morale and fuels my desire to reach new heights.

36

Periodically, I look back at all that I have already accomplished and find hope for the future.

Efficiency and time are the main benefits of an organized life.

37

My tasks are completed faster when I know what I doing in advance. An agenda even helps me to be on time.

I can keep a schedule and still enjoy my spontaneous side.

38

I allow time for outings and give myself permission to indulge in my favorite hobbies.

I spend time thinking about the path I am in and the place where I want to be.

39

Organization and order are the ingredients that make my life efficient. Having a plan makes it easier for me to maximize my time and productivity.

My appointments are clearly marked in my planner.

40

When I commit myself to an engagement, I quickly mark my calendar so I can remember it.
I store reminders in my phone and computer so I am punctual.
My agenda is with me everywhere I go so I know what is going on in my life.

I jot down a variety of lists so I remember all the things I intend to do.

41

My goals are always written somewhere visible. And yet my vision is written on my heart.

Listening to my feelings allows me to make alterations in my life.

42

When I feel overwhelmed, I take a step back from work. If I feel alone, I spend more time with my family and friends. I take a vacation when I experience exhaustion.

I have an active and busy life that I thoroughly enjoy.

43

I am able to enjoy all my activities and obligations because I take the time to plan and prepare my schedule. Because of this, I am better prepared for any unforeseen issues that arise. My careful planning allows me to fully enjoy all the activities in my life.

I invest my time and money on things of substance.

44

Periodically, I do an inventory of my time to ensure that I am devoted to what is dearest to me. Instead of waiting for some free time, I make time for what I value.

My life is focused on eternal value, not short-lived pleasures.

45

Material possessions are fleeting; therefore I focus on my relationships. I value people over possessions because people are irreplaceable.

I keep my priorities in order by devoting time to the people in my life.

46

I reflect on ways to ensure that my priorities remain in order permanently.

If I feel I'm sinking into a rut at work, I use my time management skills to rework my schedule.

47

I rearrange my tasks according to my priorities, making sure I get the most important ones accomplished. If necessary, the lesser priorities can wait.

With the right dose of pressure, I can conquer fear and self doubt.

48

I can fly over mountains and accomplish things I never would have accomplished if I worked with mediocrity instead. Limitations are feeble against me when I am on a mission.

I look at the situations in my life objectively.

49

I have outgrown the need to respond impulsively to stressful situations. Instead, I allow myself to take a step back and analyze circumstances to decide on the best course of action.

No one makes my decisions for me.

50

I am where I am because I choose to be here. If I stay here, it is my choice and I do so with an open mind and heart, yet I remain eager and ready to soak in everything I can from my current place in history.

If I decide that this situation is unhealthy or unsuitable for me, I move on.

51

I let go of the need to blame my unhappiness on my circumstances or on others. Blame has never solved my problems. I am free to change my circumstances if, after mature reflection, I decide that doing so would be my best course of action.

As I become more organized, I naturally begin to feel more responsible for my own actions.

52

Organization leads to success, and success lead to increased confidence and responsibilities.

I have the authority to remove bad habits from my agenda.

53

I can retrain my body and mind to eliminate bad habits so I can be more productive.

I am wise enough to identify when I am pressured into making a bad decision.

54

When that happens, I use my veto power to prevent myself from planting a bad seed. I am also vigilant to ensure that I don't form poor habits.

When I find a bad habit, I immediately make a plan on how to stop it.

55

I reflect regularly on my behavior in order to identify habits that may be hindering me from personal progress.

Because I have invested in organizing my life, I have a guide for my days.

56

I have a purpose and direction for my life. I am no longer a victim of circumstance but an active player in my own life.

Pressure can be my invigorating teammate.

57

My work benefits from applying gentle pressure to myself. It motivates me to do my best.

I know that I have the time to accomplish everything I desire.

58

Thinking of time as an hourglass is not representative of the way I view time. Instead, I imagine all of the sands of time spread throughout an enormous desert. I can see time extend in every direction.

I strive to organize my time effectively because I love spending time with my family.

59

I enjoy the times we have to talk and enjoy each other's company. I have an attitude that allows me to work to live and not live to work.

Life is unpredictable; therefore I try to prepare myself as best as I can.

60

My life is precious; therefore I take good care of my family and myself.

I have peace in the midst of crisis because I am secure.

61

Because I plan ahead, I enjoy the calm before the storm. I also remain calm during the storm because I know that I am protected. Even after the thunder comes to an end, I choose to be calm.

When I see a raging storm in front of me I resist the impulse to panic.

62

I remind myself that I have sunshine in my back pocket. Crisis cannot bend me out of shape because peace is my core support.

I am a beacon of hope for the people around me.

63

Having a plan available to me helps me to take care of myself and those around me. Others look to me as a role model so I remain strong in my resolve and inner peace.

I realize that anything worth doing comes with its own challenges.

64

I accept this as a normal part of life. Therefore, when obstacles present themselves, I calmly seek the best solution and take decisive action to overcome them.

I use my critical thinking skills to step back from a problem and see it from all angles.

65

I take all solutions into consideration to enable me to make the wisest decision.

I use my creativity to think outside the box.

66

Sometimes an issue can be simply sidestepped so I can move on. Other times, the challenge must be dealt with head- on before I can move forward.

My optimistic attitude steps in to provide me with workable solutions.

67

Almost every challenge comes with a benefit. When I allow myself to see it, I often realize that the issue serves a purpose after all.

Whatever the challenge, I feel that it must be there for a reason.

68

It is up to me to discover why and make the best of the moment. So I confidently step up to the plate, ready for action.

Stepping outside my comfort zone lets me expand my horizons.

69

I can learn new things, develop new skills, and discover new talents and passions I never knew I had. It brings me new joys that do not exist in my normal routine.

Every day gives me another chance to work on making myself the very best I can be.

70

I take action toward achieving my goals and, at the end of the day; I know I am one step closer to success.

No matter how far I've come, I continue to better myself.

71

I know that the sky is not the limit, but rather the beginning of a new level. I make changes today because I want to see myself living in a future free from regret.

I devote time each day to things of eternal value and I choose to be an active participant in life.

72

In turn, I seize every opportunity to learn new skills and improve myself.

My values and priorities are evident by the way I carry myself each day.

73

Recognizing that my future is not an isolated event, but the collection of individual days, I resolve to make each day count.

I am careful to form new habits that only bring me closer to the dream I have for my future.

74

In order to be productive, I am eradicating negative behaviors from my daily routine.

Any task can be broken down into manageable pieces.

75

When I am confronted with a challenge that seems insurmountable, I sit down and make a plan that divides the work into chunks that I know I can handle. I focus on the piece that is right in front of me, giving it my full attention to avoid dissipating my energy by worrying about something that has yet to come.

If the task in front of me is beyond my skill level, I am open to asking for help.

76

My greatest asset is my ability to learn and develop new skills. I am unashamed of the fact that I may need help because I see these times as opportunities to learn and grow.

Because I am determined to finish strong, I refuse to surrender to any barriers.

77

When I am faced with a wall, I have two options: I can stop and give up, or I can find another way out.

I am a brilliant individual who is fully capable of figuring things out.

78

Instead of waiting silently for someone to rescue me with an offer for help, I think of ways in which I can help myself.

The harder I work, the sweeter the victory.

79

Having to fashion my own way makes me more appreciative of the journey. I learn a lot about myself when I see the potential stored within me.

Roadblocks are only temporary.

80

There is no such thing as a dead end. My job is to find a detour in order to arrive at my goal, even if it's via a different route than I originally planned.

I am always coming up with new ideas to help me surmount the walls before me.

81

I combine courage and creativity to form the most powerful tool against opposition.

When I am focused, I am like an unstoppable machine on a mission to succeed.

82

I charge ahead with my goals clearly in view. I do whatever needs to be done in order to complete my tasks with excellence.

I make good use of my time by keeping track of my schedule.

83

I rid myself from distractions by placing myself in situations where I know I am able to stay on task.

Planning ahead helps me to manage my time wisely and feel better prepared for emergencies.

84

In order to avoid last minute emergencies that may take my focus away from my work, I make detailed plans ahead of time.

When I set goals, I stick to them.

85

I am a force to be reckoned with when my I keep my goals in sight. Ideas flow from me like water from a fountain.

When I get in my zone, I am creative and inspiring.

86

I exceed the expectations of all those around me. I am proud of the quality of work I complete when I devote my full attention to it.

When I feel frustrated with a project, I stop and take a step back.

87

By taking some time to reflect and refresh my mind, I get back on track quickly and easily.

I make sure I have a clear picture of my goal.

88

When I find myself wandering in circles, I take the time to clarify my goals and then lay out a plan.

I break my projects into manageable pieces and set mini- goals.

89

I separate them out into things I want to accomplish today, this week, or this month. Broken down in this manner, it is far easier to see my progress and to keep on track.

I recognize opportunities for growth and take them.

90

I let go of the need to see the entire route, focusing instead on aligning the present with my overall goal.

Today, the passion I have for my work keeps me focused on my goals.

91

The quality of my work is unparalleled. I am unstoppable because I choose to focus all of my attention on the task at hand.

I am confident that I am on the right path.

92

I have set my goals based on my God-given dreams and abilities. My thoughts are in line with these goals.

"Want To Achieve ANY Goal You Set? The FREE 6 Essential Steps To Achieve ANY Goal Special Report Will Show You How..."

In this Special Report you will discover...

- Exactly how many goals you should be aiming for at any one time.

- Why just visualizing your goals will have ZERO effect on whether you achieve them or not!

- Why putting your goal where you can see it all the time is a recipe for failure.

- Why the 'experts' have got it all wrong about whether you should tell people your goals or not.

- PLUS a special gift worth up to $120!

Go to www.GoalAchievementFormula.com/free

Discover more "92 Tips" and "92 Affirmations" at www.92Tips.com

"A risk isn't a risk if you know deep down that it's the next logical step for you. Just take that step and you'll never regret it."

Made in the USA
San Bernardino, CA
18 February 2013